NO LONGER PROPERTY OF
ANYTHINK LIBRARIES/
RANGEVIEW LIBRARY DISTRICT
anythink

D0623833

That's My Dog

BEAGLES

by Beth Bence Reinke

FOCUS READERS

www.focusreaders.com

Focus Readers is distributed by North Star Editions:
sales@northstareditions.com | 888-417-0195

Produced for Focus Readers by Red Line Editorial.

Photographs ©: Roy Palmer/Shutterstock Images, cover, 1; eAlisa/Shutterstock Images, 4–5; Soloviova Liudmyla/Shutterstock Images, 6; Svshot/Shutterstock Images, 8–9; Master1305/Shutterstock Images, 10; Jason DeCrow/AP Images, 13; iamsom/iStockphoto, 14–15; Dario Edigi/iStockphoto, 16, 29; Paul Wishart/Shutterstock Images, 18; Craig Ruttle/AP Images, 20–21; apisitmueanpoot/Shutterstock Images, 22–23; s5iztok/iStockphoto, 24; Aleksandar Nakic/iStockphoto, 27

ISBN
978-1-63517-538-7 (hardcover)
978-1-63517-610-0 (paperback)
978-1-63517-754-1 (ebook pdf)
978-1-63517-682-7 (hosted ebook)

Library of Congress Control Number: 2017948105

Printed in the United States of America
Mankato, MN
November, 2017

About the Author

Beth Bence Reinke is an animal lover with degrees in nutrition and biology education. Her childhood ambition of being a veterinarian was sidetracked by her cat allergy. Instead, she's a registered dietitian who writes children's books about animals, science, and nutrition. Her dog, Gabe, was a beagle mix.

TABLE OF CONTENTS

CHAPTER 1

The Busy Beagle 5

CHAPTER 2

British Roots 9

CHAPTER 3

Made for Hunting 15

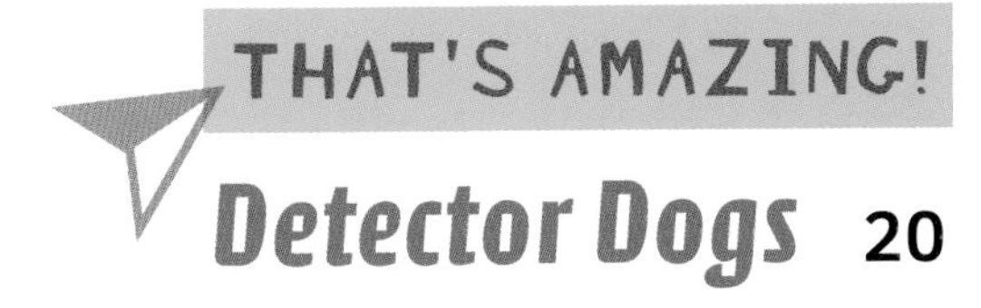

THAT'S AMAZING!

Detector Dogs 20

CHAPTER 4

Caring for a Beagle 23

Focus on Beagles • 28

Glossary • 30

To Learn More • 31

Index • 32

CHAPTER 1

THE BUSY BEAGLE

Beagles are happy dogs. They are known for their cheerful personalities. They have big eyes and gentle expressions. Beagles are not good guard dogs. This is because they are very friendly.

Beagles have a lot of energy.

A leash prevents a beagle from following smells or chasing things on a walk.

Beagles are pack dogs. That means they love to be in a group. Pet beagles think their human families are their packs. They like playing with other dogs, too. If a beagle is left alone, it may bark or howl.

Beagles love to run and chase things. They are curious, too. Beagles have a strong sense of smell. They use it to explore everything within reach. Beagles can't resist an interesting smell. Sometimes this gets them into trouble!

FUN FACT

In the 1960s, President Lyndon B. Johnson had pet beagles. Two of them were named Him and Her.

CHAPTER 2

BRITISH ROOTS

Beagles are a kind of hound. Hounds help people hunt. They have done this for hundreds of years. The beagle's **ancestors** came from Great Britain. Hunters there used beagles to hunt rabbits.

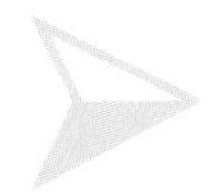

Some owners still take their beagles hunting today.

A beagle mother usually has four to six puppies at a time.

British hunters chose dogs that ran fast and had a good sense of smell. These dogs had puppies. The puppies were good hunters, too.

Soon there were many packs of hunting beagles.

In the 1870s, pairs of beagles were brought to the United States. Over time, beagles became popular with American hunters. The **breed** was **registered** by the American Kennel Club (AKC) in 1885.

FUN FACT

Pocket beagles existed long ago. They were so tiny that they could fit into people's pockets. The dogs were popular among British kings and queens.

This group keeps official lists of dog breeds and hosts **dog shows**.

Today, beagles are the most popular breed of hounds. They make fun and loyal family pets. Beagle owners can join a special club. The National Beagle Club holds contests called field trials.

FUN FACT

In 2008, a beagle named Uno won Best in Show at the Westminster Dog Show for the first time.

Uno's handler walks him in during the Westminster Dog Show.

CHAPTER 3

MADE FOR HUNTING

Beagles have lovable faces. Their foreheads are wide. They have square **muzzles**. Their ears are soft and droopy. A beagle's coat is short. It feels smooth and stiff. The coat can be several colors.

It takes a beagle puppy a little over a year to reach full size.

Most tricolor beagles are white, black, and brown.

Most beagles have a **tricolor** coat. Some have tiny spots called **ticking**.

Beagles are small dogs. They are 13 to 15 inches (33 to 38 cm) tall at the shoulder. Most beagles weigh less than 30 pounds (14 kg).

Some hounds chase things by sight. But beagles are scent hounds. They use their amazing noses to find scent trails. Because of this, beagles can track animals they can't even see.

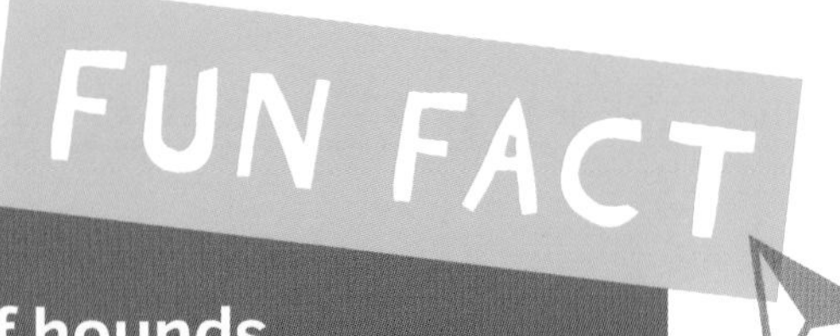

There are 27 breeds of hounds. Other kinds include basset hounds, foxhounds, and bloodhounds.

To take their beagles hunting, hunters must train the dogs well.

From head to tail, beagle bodies are made for hunting. Their sturdy legs are good for long runs. Beagle noses can't resist an interesting smell. Their large nostrils take in lots of air and scents.

The beagle's long ears help with hunting, too. As the dog sniffs along, its ears brush the ground. They stir up scents for the nose to smell. The beagle's white-tipped tail sticks up like a flag as it runs.

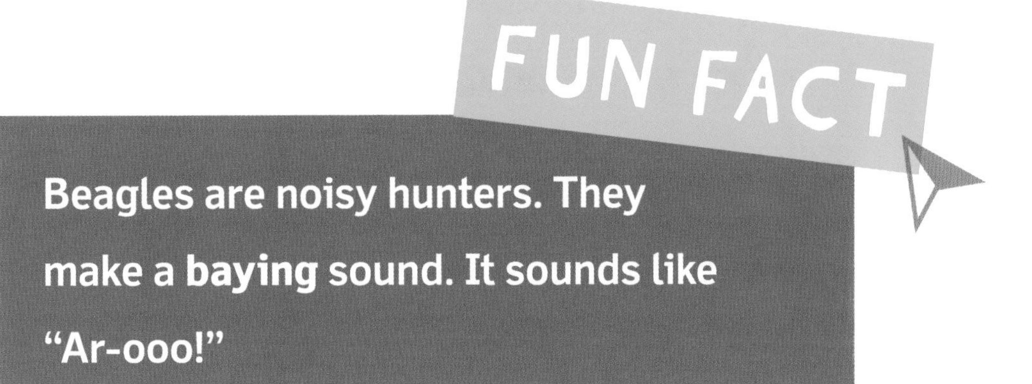

THAT'S AMAZING!

DETECTOR DOGS

Some beagles work for the US government as detector dogs. They use their noses to keep human food supplies safe.

Detector dogs and their **handlers** work in airports. The beagles smell suitcases. They sniff out illegal food and plants from other countries. These items are not allowed in the United States. The foods could bring insects or diseases that hurt crops.

If a beagle smells an illegal food or plant, he alerts his handler. The handler unzips the suitcase. The food or plant is taken away so it can't cause harm.

A detector dog works with her handler in an airport.

Protecting
American

CHAPTER 4

CARING FOR A BEAGLE

Beagles are curious, energetic dogs. They need daily exercise to use up their energy. This helps them stay calm indoors. Playing with toys keeps a beagle busy. So does going for walks.

A bored beagle may chew things.

Beagles can also be trained to do agility events such as running through tubes.

If left loose, a beagle may follow a scent and run away. Beagles should always walk on a leash. A fenced yard is useful, too. Leashes and fences keep beagles safe.

Obedience training is important. Beagles should learn to come, sit, and stay. When a beagle obeys, it deserves praise. Beagles are smart but stubborn. They pay attention only for a short time. Training beagles requires patience.

FUN FACT

The most famous beagle in the world is Snoopy. He is Charlie Brown's dog in the *Peanuts* comic strip.

Beagles are crazy about food. Treats can help with training. But beagles sometimes keep eating even after their bellies are full. Food should be measured to give the right amount. Beagles only need to be fed twice a day.

Beagles are easy to groom. Brushing twice a week gets rid of loose hair. A beagle's ears can collect wax or dirt. Gentle wiping with a damp cloth keeps them clean.

Beagles love to be with their human families.

Beagles enjoy company. They can get along with kids and other pets. Giving beagles lots of time to play and love makes them happy.

FOCUS ON

BEAGLES

Write your answers on a separate piece of paper.

1. Write an email to a friend describing what you learned about how to groom a beagle.
2. Would you like to go hunting with a beagle? Why or why not?
3. What color is the tip of a beagle's tail?
   A. white
   B. black
   C. brown
4. What might happen if a beagle found an open bag of dog food?
   A. The beagle would howl or bark.
   B. The beagle would eat too much.
   C. The beagle would run away.

5. What does **track** mean in this book?

But beagles are scent hounds. They use their amazing noses to find scent trails. Because of this, beagles can ***track*** *animals they can't even see.*

A. to walk on a path
B. to follow something
C. to run in front of something

6. What does **obedience** mean in this book?

Obedience *training is important. Beagles should learn to come, sit, and stay.*

A. the ability to jump very high
B. the ability to follow directions
C. the ability to make friends

Answer key on page 32.

GLOSSARY

ancestors
Family members from the past.

baying
A deep, long howling.

breed
A group of animals that share the same looks and features.

dog shows
Competitions where different dogs are judged based on the standard for their breed.

handlers
People who train and work with dogs.

muzzles
Animals' noses and mouths.

registered
Recorded a dog's breed and allowed it to compete in events.

ticking
Tiny spots of color on a dog's coat.

tricolor
Having three colors.

TO LEARN MORE

BOOKS

Bodden, Valerie. *Beagles*. Mankato, MN: Creative Education, 2014.

Gagne, Tammy. *Foxhounds, Coonhounds, and Other Hound Dogs*. Mankato, MN: Capstone Press, 2017.

Newman, Aline Alexander, and Gary Weitzman. *How to Speak Dog: A Guide to Decoding Dog Language*. Washington, DC: National Geographic, 2013.

NOTE TO EDUCATORS

Visit **www.focusreaders.com** to find lesson plans, activities, links, and other resources related to this title.

INDEX

A

American Kennel Club (AKC), 11

C

coat, 15–16

D

detector dogs, 20

E

ears, 19
exercise, 23

G

Great Britain, 9
groom, 26

H

height, 16–17
hounds, 9, 12, 17
hunt, 9–11, 18–19

J

Johnson, Lyndon B., 7

N

National Beagle Club, 12

P

pack, 6, 11
Peanuts, 25
personalities, 5
pocket beagles, 11

S

smell, 7, 10, 17–20

T

training, 25–26

U

United States, 11, 20

W

weight, 17

Answer Key: 1. Answers will vary; **2.** Answers will vary; **3.** A; **4.** B; **5.** B; **6.** B